► **The New American History**

SERIES
EDITED
BY
ERIC FONER

Beneficiaries of
English Colonies

by

American

Catastrophe: The in America

John M. Murrin

Historical Association

JOHN M. MURRIN, Professor of History at Princeton University, is co-editor of *Saints and Revolutionaries: Essays on Early American History* (Norton, 1984) and the 1986–87 winner of the Society of Cincinnati (New Jersey chapter) Award for his work on the history of colonial New Jersey.

This essay originally appeared in *The New American History,* published by Temple University Press in the series Critical Perspectives on the Past, edited by Susan Porter Benson, Stephen Brier, and Roy Rosenzweig. Copyright © 1990 Temple University.

This edition published by the American Historical Association
ISBN: 0-87229-051-4
Printed in the United States of America

▶ Contents

▶ **Essays in** *The New American History* **series**

▶ Introduction

IN THE COURSE OF THE PAST TWENTY YEARS, AMERICAN HISTORY HAS BEEN remade. Inspired initially by the social movements of the 1960s and 1970s—which shattered the "consensus" vision that had dominated historical writing—and influenced by new methods borrowed from other disciplines, American historians redefined the very nature of historical study. The rise of the "new histories," the emphasis on the experience of ordinary Americans, the impact of quantification and cultural analysis, the eclipse of conventional political and intellectual history—these trends are now so widely known (and the subject of such controversy) that they need little reiteration. The study of American history today looks far different than it did a generation ago.

This series comprises essays written by thirteen scholars—many of whom have been at the forefront of the transformation of historical study—each assessing recent developments in historians' understanding of a period or a major theme in the nation's past. The idea for the collection originated with a request from the American Historical Association for a series of pamphlets addressed specifically to high school teachers of American history and designed to familiarize them with the most up-to-date historical scholarship.

ERIC FONER

After a false start or two the proposal, somewhat revised, was adopted and published as a collection by Temple University Press, and now, separately, by the AHA. *The New American History* is addressed to a wide audience: students, teachers, and the broad public concerned with the current state of American historical study.

Each author was given a free hand in developing his or her reflections. No attempt has been made to fit the essays into a predetermined mold or impose a single point of view or interpretive framework. Nonetheless, certain themes recur with remarkable regularity, demonstrating how pervasively the "new histories" have reshaped our understanding of the American past.

If anything is characteristic of the recent study of American history, it is attention to the experience of previously neglected groups—not simply as an addition to a preexisting body of knowledge but as a fundamental redefinition of history itself. Women's history has greatly expanded its subject area, moving beyond the movement for suffrage, which preoccupied earlier women historians, into such previously ignored realms as the history of sexuality. Labor history, from a field that defined its subject as the experience of wage workers in factories and the activities of unionized workers, has expanded to encompass the study of slaves, women at home, and the majority of laborers, who in America have always been unorganized.

Even more striking, perhaps, is that African-American history and women's history have matured to the point where they are not widely recognized as legitimate subfields with their own paradigms and debates but are seen as indispensable to any understanding of the broad American experience. These points are made effectively in surveys of the two fields by Thomas Holt and Linda Gordon, but they are evident in other contributions as well. Richard McCormick makes clear that any calculus of Americans' gains and losses in the late nineteenth and early twentieth centuries must take into account the severe reverses suffered by blacks in those years. William Chafe places the civil rights movement at the center of his analysis of social change in post–World War II America. My own essay on the Civil War era argues not only that slavery and emancipation were the central issues in the sectional crisis but that blacks were active agents in shaping the era's history.

Women's history, too, has forced historians not simply to compensate for their previous neglect of one-half of the population but to rethink some of their basic premises. Linda Kerber delineates how the

American Revolution affected prevailing definitions of "manhood" and "womanhood" and how patriarchy itself was restructured as a result of the revolutionary crisis. Leon Fink emphasizes the obvious but long-ignored fact that women have always been part of the country's labor history. Sean Wilentz shows that a key result of economic changes in the Jacksonian era was an ideological division between the public sphere of men and the private sphere of women.

Many of the essays also demonstrate the impact of new methods on recent historical study. John Murrin shows how historical demography has yielded a new estimate of the human toll exacted by the colonization of the New World and how epidemiology affects our understanding of the decimation of the hemisphere's original inhabitants. Alice Kessler-Harris outlines the ways in which the "new empiricism" of statistical analysis has helped shape developments in social history. Richard McCormick and Alan Brinkley assess the impact of modernization theory on the study of both pre– and post–World War I periods.

Despite the apparent ascendancy of social history, these essays do not lend credence to recent complaints that historians are no longer concerned with politics, economics, the Constitution, and intellectual history. Such traditional concerns appear in virtually every essay, although often in forms that earlier historians might find unrecognizable. The old "presidential synthesis"—which understood the evolution of American society chiefly via presidential elections and administrations—is dead (and not lamented). And "politics" now means much more than the activities of party leaders. Some essays devote attention to the broad political culture or "public life" of a particular era; others stress the role of the state itself in American history and the ways various groups have tried to use it for their own purposes.

Alan Brinkley, for example, discusses the New Deal within the context of the constraints imposed on government by the nature of America's political and economic institutions, and the general impact of the period on the evolution of the American state. And Walter LaFeber shows how the Constitution has helped to shape the evolution of American foreign policy.

Many historians have lamented of late the failure of the current generation of scholars to produce a modern "synthesis" of the American past. Older synthetic interpretations, ranging from Frederick Jackson Turner's frontier thesis to the consensus view of the 1950s, have been shattered, but no new one has emerged to fill the void. Indeed, the very diversity of the "new histories" and the portrait of America they have created seem to have fragmented historical scholarship and impeded the attempt to create a coherent new vision of the national experience. Several of the essays echo this concern, but there is sufficient similarity in their approaches and interpretations to suggest that the fragmentation of historical study may have been overstated. If the essays do not, and by their very nature cannot, produce the widely called-for new synthesis, several do point in that direction. Sean Wilentz, for example, suggests that the social, political, and economic history of Jacksonian America can be integrated into a coherent whole by placing the market revolution at the center of the account. McCormick demonstrates that a "public life" can be a flexible, imaginative concept, capable of integrating a variety of social, economic, and political developments.

As this series demonstrates, American history is a field of remarkable diversity and vitality. Its practitioners continue to grapple with the most pressing issues and persistent themes of our national experience: definitions of liberty and equality, causes of social change, the exercise of political power. Today, popular knowledge—or lack of knowledge—of the nation's past has once again become a subject of intense public discussion. Certainly, the more all of us—students, teachers, and other citizens—know of our national experience, the better. But as these essays illustrate, American history at its best remains not simply a collection of facts, not a politically sanctioned listing of indisputable "truths," but an ongoing mode of collective self-discovery about the nature of our society.

ERIC FONER
Columbia University

▶ ▶ ▶ ▶ ▶ ▶ ▶ ▶ ▶ ▶ ▶ ▶ ▶ ▶ ▶

BENEFICIARIES OF CATASTROPHE: THE ENGLISH COLONIES IN AMERICA

John M. Murrin

MOST AMERICANS REGARD OUR COLONIAL ERA AS A HEROIC PERIOD. BOLD MEN and women, often fired by a sense of divine mission or by a quest for a fuller and juster life than Europe could offer, braved the severities of an Atlantic crossing, attacked the "howling wilderness," erected their tiny settlements, established large and thriving families, and somehow still found time to create the free institutions that remain even today the basis for our democratic society. Eighteenth-century Europeans saw things differently. The generation that witnessed the American Revolution also debated the moral significance of the discovery of the Americas and the establishment of European trade and settlement in both the East and West Indies. Abbé Guillaume Thomas François Raynal in France and Dr. William Robertson in Scotland found little to praise and much to condemn. "I dare to state it," agreed Joseph Mandrillon, a minor philosophe, "the discovery of America was an evil. Never can the advantages it brought about (no matter how one considers or depicts them) compensate for the harm it has caused." To educated and thoughtful Europeans, the opening of the Americas seemed one of the greatest moral monstrosities of all time.

The philosophes estimated that the conquest and settlement of the Americas cost the lives of some twenty million people, most of them Amerindians. They admitted that the process led to swift improvements in navi-

1

gational techniques, shipbuilding, mapmaking, and related skills and that it certainly quickened the pace of European commerce. But, they insisted, most of these positive assets were used only to exchange vices between the hemispheres. Europeans carried cruelty, greed, slaves and enslavement, disease and death to the Americas. They brought back syphilis, gold and silver to fuel inflation and an interminable cycle of destructive wars, and such products as tobacco and sugar to undermine the health of people who never even got close to the New World. Early America was a catastrophe —a horror story, not an epic.

America's revolutionary leaders—such as Benjamin Franklin and Thomas Jefferson, who both served the new republic as ministers to the court of Louis XVI—resented these arguments and the related claim that the environment of the New World was so enfeebling that, over time, it caused all forms of life to degenerate. American plants and animals had less variety and vitality than those of Europe, Asia, or Africa, insisted most careful observers, who were particularly struck by the paucity of large mammals in the Western Hemisphere. Humans who moved to the Americas would surely inflict the same degeneracy upon their descendants, the philosophes warned. Jefferson once met this criticism by persuading a friend to ship a moose to France as a typical example of an American deer. But European sentiment was already beginning to shift by then. Many philosophes readily conceded that the American Revolution might herald a daring new departure for all mankind. Its message of liberty and equality, constitutionalism married to popular sovereignty, reverberated throughout much of Europe. Indeed, the success of the revolution ended the debate over whether America was a hideous mistake, or at least banished that perception to what is now the Third World. Even historians usually regard this controversy as more amusing than instructive.

Until recently, American colonial history recounted the activities of Europeans in America: the institutions they established, the liberties they fought to secure, the ideas they propounded about God, man, and society. But as in other fields of American history, since the 1960s scholars have turned to large problems of social history. Who were the settlers? Where did they come from? What sorts of communities did they struggle to create? Who was here when they arrived? Where did the colonists get their slaves? What happened when these very different cultures came together?

Research in elementary numbers during the 1970s and 1980s ought to revive the Enlightenment controversy about early America. Reasonable estimates now exist for the flow of people across the Atlantic, including the volume of the African slave trade from the fifteenth through the nineteenth century. Some of the most imaginative scholarship of the past generation has gone into reconstructing the approximate size of the pre-Columbian Indian population in several major portions of the Americas, a necessary prelude to measuring the impact of European intrusion. Together these materials tell a story a good deal more dismal than even the philosophes had quite imagined.

The figure of twenty million dead falls far short of the true total, which was at least double and perhaps triple that number. Of course, many Europeans on both the eastern and western shores of the Atlantic benefited immensely from the settlement process. Most actors on all sides of the transatlantic drama made rational choices in their own best interests, including even the slaves, once they understood what few options they still retained. But using the elementary utilitarian criterion of the greatest good for the greatest number as a crude but revealing way of assessing the overall process, nobody can now make a compelling case that the settlement of the Americas was a net benefit to mankind until sometime in the nineteenth century. In aggregate terms, losers far outnumbered winners until then. Unlike the philosophes, today's historians see what happened in early America not as a moralistic melodrama but as a tragedy of such huge proportions that one's imagination cannot easily encompass it all. The truest villains were microbes, whose predations acquired an inevitable momentum that quickly made human motivation all but irrelevant for the deadliest part of the process.

Before 1820 about eleven million people crossed the Atlantic from Europe and Africa to the Caribbean, North America, and South America. The overwhelming majority, about eight million, came against their will —in chains. African slaves constituted almost three-fourths of the entire migration. Only in the period between 1820 and 1840 would the number of free passengers catch up with and then decisively surpass the volume of the slave trade throughout the Atlantic world. For more than three centuries, in other words, the slave trade was no unfortunate excess on the periphery of free migration. It was the norm.

The situation was less extreme in the English colonies, at least on the mainland, than elsewhere. About 380,000 people left the British Isles for England's North American and Caribbean colonies before 1700. A huge majority came from England and Wales, not Scotland or Ireland. They were joined by 10,000 or more other Europeans, mostly from the Netherlands and France. During the seventeenth century almost 350,000 slaves, or about 47 percent of the people crossing the Atlantic to the English colonies, left Africa to provide coerced labor for these new societies. Three-fourths of the entire human wave went to the West Indies, which attracted over 220,000 settlers (roughly 56 percent of the Europeans) and nearly 320,000 slaves (about 91 percent of the Africans). The Chesapeake colonies drew nearly 120,000 settlers (32 percent) and at least 25,000 slaves (7 percent). The Middle Atlantic region claimed a net of some 20,000 colonists (just over 5 percent) and a few thousand slaves. After outmigrants are subtracted, probably fewer than 20,000 Europeans and an insignificant trickle of Africans went to New England.

Patterns changed during the eighteenth century. The African slave trade hit its all-time peak as over 6.1 million people were dragged aboard ships headed for the Americas—nearly 45 percent of them traveling in British or American vessels. Losses in transit probably approached or exceeded 20 percent until at least midcentury but improved somewhat after that. Slaves were not the only unwilling migrants. Between 1718 and 1775 Great Britain shipped 50,000 convicts to North America, most of them to Maryland or Virginia.

Recent estimates indicate that between 150,000 and 230,000 Europeans entered the mainland colonies from 1700 to 1760, fairly close to the probable minimum of 180,000 slaves imported during the same period. Most of the voluntary immigrants came from new sources in the eighteenth century. Between 1700 and 1760 nearly 60,000 Germans and more than 30,000 Irish settlers and servants sailed for the Delaware Valley alone. Thousands of others—Irish, Scottish, English, and German—landed in New York, the Chesapeake, and the lower South. London registration records indicate that the British capital continued to send perhaps 800 indentured servants to the colonies per year from 1718 to 1759. No doubt the capital and the home counties provided other migrants as well. Northern England probably contributed a sizable (as yet untabulated) stream.

After the fall of New France in 1760, immigration exploded: 55,000 Irish, 40,000 Scots, 30,000 English, 12,000 Germans, and 84,500 slaves swarmed into North America. Totaling more than 220,000 people, the newcomers equaled nearly a seventh of the total population of just under 1.6 million people in the mainland colonies in 1760. Their story—where they came from and how they got to America—has been marvelously told in Bernard Bailyn's Pulitzer Prize–winning study, *Voyagers to the West* (1986). The typical colonist from southern England was an unmarried male in his teens or early twenties who often possessed artisanal skills and brought with him a set of optimistic expectations. He was most likely to settle in Virginia or Maryland, and he probably left home because of the pull of the New World, not out of exasperation with England. The characteristic emigré from north Britain (Ulster, Scotland, and northern England) sailed to America as part of an intact family. The head of the household was typically in his thirties, was frequently a farmer, and carried bitter memories of the social environment he was leaving—heavy taxes, rack-renting landlords, unemployment or underemployment. He usually led his family to Pennsylvania, New York, or North Carolina.

Statistically, the British colonial world as a whole approximated the dismal norm set by other Atlantic empires in the eighteenth century. Over 1.5 million slaves left Africa for British colonies in the West Indies and

North America, outnumbering by three to one the half-million free migrants who sailed for the same provinces. In the islands, however, slave imports overwhelmed free immigrants by about ten to one. On the mainland, slaves probably outnumbered other newcomers in most decades between 1700 and 1760, but for the continent and the century as a whole, free migrants exceeded slaves by a margin of roughly four to three over the entire period, with most of the edge for voluntary migrants coming after 1760.

Settlers and slaves carried with them microbes that were far more deadly than muskets and cannon to Indian peoples with virtually no immunities to smallpox, measles, and even simple bronchial infections. The result was the greatest known demographic catastrophe in the history of the world, a population loss that usually reached or exceeded 90 percent in any given region within a century of contact with the invaders. In warm coastal areas such as the West Indies and much of Brazil, it approached complete extinction in a much shorter time. By Russell Thornton's careful estimates, the pre-Columbian population of the Americas exceeded 70 million, or about one-seventh of the 500 million people then inhabiting the globe; high estimates for the Americas run to double this number. Mexico probably had more than 20 million when Hernan Cortés arrived in 1519, Peru from 8 to 12 million, the Caribbean at least 10 million (some estimates run much higher), the continent north of the Rio Grande close to 8 million (with about 5.7 million in what is now the lower forty-eight states), Brazil over 3 million, and the rest of South America several million more. By comparison, Europe east of the Urals probably had about 55 million people in 1500—living, to be sure, in a much smaller geographical area. The Indian population of 1492 thus outnumbered all European immigrants to 1820 by a ratio of perhaps twenty-five to one and all the Africans who arrived by maybe nine to one.

Disease demolished these numerical advantages. The Carib Indians had virtually disappeared from the Greater Antilles by 1550. Mexico's 20 million had plummeted to 730,000 by 1620, and Peru's 10 million to 600,000. The Americas were never a "virgin land"; in Francis Jennings's melancholy but telling phrase, they became a "widowed land." By the mid-eighteenth century Europeans outnumbered Africans except in Brazil, the West Indies, and South Carolina, but nearly everywhere south of Pennsylvania (except in Mexico and a few other localities that did not rely heavily on African slavery) blacks outnumbered Indians within regions of European settlement.

Interaction among the three cultures was extensive. The plants and animals of the Western Hemisphere seemed so strange to Europeans that without knowledgeable occupants to tell them what was edible and how it could be prepared, the intruders would have found far greater difficulty in surviving. The first explorers or settlers to arrive in a region, for instance, nearly always had to barter for food. Indian trails showed them the easiest ways to get from one place to another and where to portage streams and rivers. Indian canoes and snowshoes displayed an ingenuity and utility that Europeans quickly borrowed. Settlers also learned from their slaves. Africans, for example, may well have taught South Carolina planters how to cultivate rice. From their masters, in turn, Africans acquired knowledge of the prevailing European language and, more slowly, Christian convictions.

For their part, Indians greatly valued firearms whenever they could get them. Those who acquired them early, such as the Iroquois, won huge advantages over neighboring tribes. Indian women quickly discovered the benefits of European pots, but imported textiles took longer to find Indian markets. Not so alcohol. It exacted a fierce toll from a people who had no cultural experience with its intoxicating powers.

Yet Indian society had many built-in immunities to European influences. Although most Indian tribes in North America were agricultural, they also spent part of the year hunting. Their crops gave them a strong attachment to the land but not the European sense of exclusive ownership of individual plots. The need to move every year also prevented Indians from developing large permanent dwellings and necessarily restricted their desire and capacity to consume European goods. Because women erected and controlled the home environment (wigwam, tepee, or longhouse in North America), they had no wish to own any more products than they were willing to lug from one place to another several times a year. Women also did the routine agricultural labor in Indian societies, a practice that seemed degrading to male European observers. The consequences of their attitude were significant: however well intentioned, European efforts to "civilize" the Indians by converting warriors into farmers seldom succeeded, for at the deepest cultural level these demands amounted to nothing less than an attempt to turn men into women. When Indians did copy the agricultural practices of the settlers, slavery often provided a necessary intermediating mechanism. Nineteenth-century Cherokee warriors, for instance, were willing to become planters who forced other men to work for them in the fields.

War provided a grisly but frequent point of cultural contact, and perhaps no activity did more to intensify mutual misunderstanding. European geopolitical norms had little resonance among Indians, who were far more likely to fight for captives than for territory or trade. Aztecs waged continuous war to provide thousands of sacrifices for their gods every year. Most North American Indians practiced analogous rites but on a much smaller scale, and they were far more likely to keep their prisoners. Indeed, Indians often fought in order to replace losses by death, a phenomenon called "the mourning war." Epidemics, which utterly demoralized some tribes, accelerated warfare among others, such as the Iroquois in the northern or the Catawba in the deep southern region of what is now the United States. As the death toll from imported disease climbed at appalling rates, these tribes struggled to make up for their losses.

In the process Indian societies proved far more openly assimilationist than European colonies were. The Iroquois, for example, seem to have begun by absorbing such similar neighbors as the Hurons and other tribes who spoke Iroquoian dialects. When that supply ran thin, the Iroquois turned to Algonquian tribes. As early as the 1650s or 1660s, most of the people who claimed to be members of the Five Nations of the Iroquois Confederation had not been born Iroquois. They were adoptees. Only in this way could the confederacy preserve its numbers and its strength. Even this strategy was failing by the 1690s, when virtually all potential enemies had equal access to muskets and gunpowder, and the price of war became heavier than its benefits. In 1701 the Five Nations chose a policy of neutrality toward both the English and the French, and thereafter they usually confined their wars with other Indians to fighting distant southerly tribes.

During the eighteenth century some Indian communities adopted significant numbers of Europeans and granted them and their descendants full equality with other members of the tribe. Women usually decided which captives to adopt and which to execute, often after deliberate torture. Most of those tortured and killed were adult men; most of those adopted were women and children, whether Europeans or other Indians. European women who spent a year or more in captivity quite often made a voluntary choice to remain. This decision baffled and dismayed the European men they left behind, including in many cases a husband and children. Adult male settlers found it inexplicable that "civilized" women, some of whom were even church members in full communion, could actually prefer a "savage" life and would not object to toiling in the fields. In fact, Indian women enjoyed greater respect within their tribes than European housewives received from their own communities, and Indian women worked fewer hours and participated more openly in making important decisions, including questions of war and peace. Adoptees shared fully in these benefits; some adopted males even became chiefs.

On the other hand, Indian fondness for torture shocked and enraged most settlers. Warriors took pride in their ability to withstand the most excruciating torment without complaint. The ideal brave chanted defiant war songs or hurled verbal abuse at his tormentors until the end. Europeans, who did not share these values, screamed horribly, wept, and begged for mercy until they finally died. But their people nearly always won the war. From an Indian perspective, the weak were indeed inheriting the earth.

Europeans were accustomed to fighting for trade and territory; unlike

Indians, they showed almost no inclination to capture opponents, adopt them, and assimilate them fully into their culture. Their Indian captives became slaves instead and seldom lived long. Exceptions to this pattern did occur, though rarely as a result of war. On Martha's Vineyard and Nantucket, for instance, most Indians did convert to Christianity in the seventeenth century, and in the eighteenth—until disease radically diminished their numbers—many of them went to sea as skilled harpoonists on whaling vessels.

Such examples of peaceful cooperation and borrowing did little to mitigate the ferocity of war when it occurred. Because the settlers regarded themselves as "civilized" and all Indians as "savages," they saw little point in observing their lingering rules of chivalry in these conflicts. Often encumbered in the early years by armor and heavy weapons, they could not keep up with Indian warriors in the wilderness and were not very skillful at tracking opponents through dense forest. But they could find the Indians' villages, burn them, and destroy their crops. In early Virginia, New England, and New Netherland, the intruders—not the Indians—introduced the tactic of the deliberate and systematic massacre of a whole community, which usually meant the women, children, and elderly who had been left behind when the warriors took to the forest. The intruders went even further. Often women and children became their targets of choice, as in the Mystic River campaign of 1637 during the Pequot War, when Puritan soldiers ignored a fort manned by warriors to incinerate another a few miles away, which was packed with the tribe's noncombatants. The motive for this kind of warfare was not at all mysterious. It was not genocide in any systematic sense; settlers relied too heavily on Indians to try to get rid of all of them. The real purpose was terror. Outnumbered in a hostile land, Europeans used deliberate terror against one tribe to send a grisly warning to all others nearby. This practice struck the Indians as at least as horrible and senseless as torture seemed to the Europeans, but it could be grimly effective. Most American colonies were founded by terrorists.

Americans like to see their history as a chronicle of progress. Indeed it is. Considering how it began, it could only improve. The internal development of the settler communities is a story of growth and innovation. Ordinary free families in the English colonies achieved a level of economic autonomy and well-being difficult to match anywhere else at that time. Starvation, for example, was never a problem after the very early years, but it continued to threaten most other communities around the world. The main reason for the contrast was, of course, the availability of land in North America, which made subsistence relatively simple once the newcomers understood what crops to grow. It also tended to make younger sons the equals of the eldest, because in most families they could all expect to inherit land.

Before 1700, however, the human cost was immense for most colonists, and it got much worse for Africans in the eighteenth century, the period in which the Atlantic slave trade peaked. Cheap land meant scarce labor—the same principle that liberated Europeans enslaved Africans—and the coercion of outsiders became the most obvious answer to the shortage. The quest for material improvement motivated the vast majority of settlers and servants who crossed the ocean, and they had few scruples about depriving outsiders of their liberty in order to achieve their own goals. That is, they did in America what they would not have dared try in Europe; they enslaved other people. Even Puritans and Quakers, driven by powerful religious commitments, found prosperity quite easy to bear. To the extent that they resisted slavery, they acted less from principle than from a dislike of "strangers" who might cause them moral difficulties.

Historians have worked with patience and imagination to reconstruct the community life of English North America. Paying close attention to settler motivation, demography, family structure, community organization, local economy, and social values, they have uncovered not just a single "American" colonial experience but an amazing variety of patterns. Current scholarship is now beginning to link this diversity to specific regional subcultures within the British Isles and their expansion and even intensification in North America.

Here too the numbers are striking, particularly the contrast between those who came and those who survived. Within the English colonies before 1700, the huge majority of settlers that chose the West Indies over the mainland had become a distinct minority by century's end. The 220,000 Europeans and 320,000 slaves who had sailed for the islands left a total of fewer than 150,000 survivors by 1700, and the preponderance of slaves over free colonists, which already exceeded three to one, grew more overwhelming with each passing year. The 120,000 Europeans and at least 25,000 slaves who had gone to the southern mainland colonies before 1700 had just over 100,000 survivors at that date. By contrast, only 40,000 people had gone to the Middle Atlantic and New England colonies in the seventeenth century, but the survivors and their descendants numbered almost 150,000 by 1700, just over 5,000 of whom were slaves. Founded by some 10 percent of the free migration stream and only 5 or 6 percent of the total number of free and enslaved passengers, by 1700 the northern colonies accounted for considerably more than half of all the European settlers in English North America and the West Indies. This sudden and quite unexpected expansion of the area of free-labor settlement was the greatest anomaly yet in two centuries of European overseas expansion. The Middle Atlantic colonies in particular, which had gotten off to a slower start than New England, were by 1700 poised to become the fastest-growing region on the continent and probably in the world over the next century and a half.

One paradox is striking. Almost certainly, intense religious motivation was underrepresented among those leaving the British Isles. The Puritans, Quakers, and other religious exiles were a tiny percentage of the transatlantic migration, but their coreligionists who remained at home were numerous enough to generate a revolution and execute a king between 1640 and 1660. Protestant dissent acquired its power in American life not because of its prominence among the migrants in general but because of the amazing ability of this small number of people to survive and multiply.

These enormous differences in rates of population growth stemmed from patterns of migration, family structure, and general health. Among the colonists, sex ratios tended to get more unbalanced the farther south one went. Men outnumbered women by only about three to two among the first settlers of New England, most of whom arrived as parts of organized families. In New Netherland the ratio was two to one, and it was probably somewhat lower in Pennsylvania. Early Maryland and Virginia attracted perhaps six men for every woman, a ratio that fell slowly. Because most Chesapeake women arrived as indentured servants, they were not legally free to marry and bear children until they had completed their terms. Most were in their mid-twenties before they could start to raise legitimate families. Not surprisingly, both the bastardy rate and the percentage of pregnant brides were quite high, cumulatively affecting something like half of all immigrant servant women. In the early West Indies, women were even scarcer, sometimes outnumbered by ten or twenty to one. To move from that situation to all-male buccaneering communities, as in Tortuga and parts of Jamaica in the 1650s and 1660s and in the Bahamas later on, did not require a radical transition.

Life expectancy and rates of natural increase also declined from north to south. The New England population became self-sustaining during the first decade after the founding of Boston in 1630. Immigration virtually ceased after 1641, and for the rest of the colonial period the region exported more people than it imported. Yet its population grew at an explosive rate from 20,000 founders to nearly 100,000 descendants in fewer than seventy years. New Netherland entered a similar cycle of rapid natural increase in the 1650s. Early New Jersey townships and Pennsylvania's first farming communities were almost certainly demographically self-sustaining from the decade of their founding, between the 1660s and 1680s.

By contrast, the Chesapeake colonies took most of the century to achieve natural growth. Although settled longer than any other part of North America, Virginia remained a colony dominated by immigrants until the decade after 1700, when native-born men (those born after 1680) finally took charge. Immigrants had already survived childhood diseases in England, but their life expectancy as young adults in the Chesapeake was much lower than that of Englishmen of the same age who stayed behind or those who went to more northerly colonies. Men could expect to live only to about age forty-five in Maryland and Virginia, and women died even sooner, especially if they were exposed to malaria while pregnant. This situation improved slowly as, for example, settlers planted orchards and replaced local drinking water with cider, and as a native-born population with improved immunities gradually replaced the immigrants. In the West Indies, life expectancy may have been as much as five years shorter. From the Chesapeake through the islands, even the men in power were often quite youthful.

These differences powerfully affected family size and structure. Although New England women married only slightly younger than their English counterparts, they averaged one or two more pregnancies per marriage, fewer died in childbirth, and they lost fewer of their children to disease. Thus eighteen of Andover's twenty-nine founding families had at least four sons who survived to age twenty-one, and fourteen of these twenty-nine families had at least four daughters who lived that long. The average age at death for the heads of these households was 71.8 years, and a third of them lived past eighty.

As these settlements matured, power gravitated naturally to their founders, who, as respectable grandfathers, continued to run most towns until the 1670s and even the 1680s. They often retained economic control over adult sons by withholding land titles until their own deaths, by which time their oldest children could be middle-aged or even elderly. They retained religious control, at least in the Massachusetts and New Haven colonies, by tying voting rights to church membership and by insisting on a publicly verified conversion experience before granting that membership. Most ministers and magistrates (the Puritan gentry who administered justice) favored a degree of compromise on this question. What later came to be called the Halfway Covenant, a measure approved by a New England synod in 1662, encouraged second-generation settlers to have their children baptized even though neither the father nor mother had yet experienced conversion. But lay saints—the grandparents who still numerically dominated most churches—resisted the implementation of this policy. They believed in infant baptism, but only for the children of proven saints. Thus very few people took advantage of the device until the founding generation began to die and lose control in the decade after King Philip's War (1675–76).

In brief, New England families tended to be patriarchal, authoritarian, and severely disciplined at the same time that New England villages were a fairly egalitarian community of aging farmers. Few of them were inclined to tolerate any significant degree of religious nonconformity. Those who could not accept local standards often made their way to Rhode Island, where they explored the difficulties of trying to find some basis for unity other than sheer dissent. It took time.

In the Delaware Valley, Quaker families shared many of the demographic characteristics of New England Puritans, but the family ethos was very different. Far less troubled by the doctrine of original sin, Quakers tried to protect the "innocence" of their numerous youngsters and give them a warm and nurturing environment. This goal included the acquisition of enough property to give each son a basis for genuine independence at a fairly youthful age and each daughter an early dowery. Quakers amassed more land and built larger and more comfortable houses than either their Anglican neighbors or the New Englanders. Those who failed to achieve these goals had difficulty marrying their children to other Quakers and themselves lost status within the Society of Friends.

The colonies created largely by Quakers—the provinces of West New Jersey and Pennsylvania—were far less authoritarian and patriarchal than those in New England. Quakers did not suppress religious dissent except occasionally within their own midst. As pacifists, they objected to any formal military institutions, and the Pennsylvania government created none until the 1750s. But the governor, who had to deal on a regular basis with a war-making British government, was seldom a Quaker. He did not easily win deference or respect from the members of the Society of Friends who continued to dominate the assembly, and who insisted on winning for it a body of privileges that greatly exceeded those claimed even by the British House of Commons, but then seldom converted these powers into actual legislation. Quaker assemblymen were far less interested in making laws than in preventing others from using the powers of government against their constituents. Even the court system existed overwhelmingly for the use of non-Quakers, and taxes remained low to nonexistent. Pennsylvania acquired its reputation as the world's best poor man's country while almost abolishing everything that the eighteenth century understood by government—the ability to wage war, pass laws, settle disputes, punish crimes, and collect taxes.

Family structure in the Chesapeake colonies differed greatly from either of these patterns. Unbalanced sex ratios before 1700 and short life expectancy even into the eighteenth century meant that almost no settlers lived to see their grandchildren. Among indentured servants arriving during the seventeenth century, many men never married at all, and others had to wait until their late twenties or thirties. Servant women also married late, but as the native-born population came of age and grew in size, its women married very young, usually in their middle to late teens. A typical seventeenth-century marriage endured only seven or eight years before one of the partners died, often leaving the surviving spouse in charge of the property and thus in a strong position to remarry. Death might also dissolve the second marriage before the oldest child by the first one had reached adulthood. Although the experience was not typical, a child could grow up in one household but by age twenty-one not even be related by blood to the husband and wife then running the family. Under these conditions, Chesapeake families tended to spread their loyalties among broader kinship networks. Uncles, aunts, cousins, and in-laws could make a real difference to an orphan's prospects. Even the local tradition of lavish hospitality to visitors may have derived some of its intensity from these imperatives.

Although the organizers of both Virginia and Maryland believed in a hierarchical and deferential social and political order, demographic realities retarded its development. True dynasties of great planters began to take shape only as the seventeenth century faded into the eighteenth. The slave population became demographically self-sustaining about a generation later than the European and thereafter multiplied almost as rapidly, a phenomenon that made the American South unique among Europe's overseas empires. Only as this process neared maturity could a planter be reasonably certain of passing on property, prestige, and authority to a lineal son. Not even then was he likely to retain significant power over the lives of his adult children. Until the age of the American Revolution, he was not likely to live that long.

Yet the men who governed seventeenth-century Virginia achieved considerable success in holding the colony to at least an elementary Anglican loyalty. Maryland, by contrast, officially favored toleration under the Roman Catholic dynasty of the Calvert family, until Anglicans finally gained control in the 1690s and established their church. In the West Indies the Church of England also became an established institution, but contemporary commentators thought that its moral hold on the planters was rather weak. Mostly because sugar was a more lucrative crop than tobacco, while the supply of land was much more limited than on the mainland, extremes of wealth emerged early in the Caribbean. Slavery was already becoming well entrenched by the 1650s, and by the end of the century the richest planters were beginning to flee back to England to live affluently as absentees off their island incomes.

Regional differences extended to ethnicity as well. New England may have been more English than England, a country that had sizable Scottish, Irish, Welsh, French Huguenot, and Dutch Reformed minorities. The Middle Atlantic region was more diverse than England. It threw together most of the people of northwestern Europe, who learned, particularly in New York, that every available formula for active government was likely to antagonize one group or another. Pennsylvania's prescription of minimal government for everyone worked better to preserve ethnic peace until war with frontier Indians threatened to tear the province apart between 1754 and 1764. The Chesapeake settlers, while predominantly English in both tidewater and piedmont, contained sizable ethnic minorities from continental Europe and, in the back country, large Scottish and Irish contingents. But after 1700 their most significant minority was African. The southern colonies mixed not just European peoples but newcomers from different continents. Slaves came to constitute about 40 percent of Virginia's population in the late colonial era. In coastal South Carolina, Africans had become a majority of two to one by the 1720s, but not even South Carolina approached the huge African preponderances of the sugar islands.

The economies of these regions also varied from north to south. In somewhat different ways, New England and the Middle Atlantic colonies largely replicated the economies of northern Europe in their urban-rural mixture, their considerable variety of local crafts, and their reliance on either fish or cereal crops as a major export. Within the Atlantic colonial world these free-labor societies were unique, but they could not have sustained themselves without extensive trade with the more typical staple colonies to the south. New Englanders learned as early as the 1640s that they needed the islands to sustain their own economy, a process that would eventually draw Rhode Islanders into the slave trade in a major way. Tobacco, rice, and sugar—all grown by forms of unfree labor—shaped Chesapeake, South Carolina, and Caribbean society in profound, almost deterministic ways.

In effect, then, the colonists sorted themselves into a broad spectrum of settlements with striking and measurable differences between one region and its neighbors. All retained major portions of their English heritage and discarded others, but what one region kept, another often scorned. David Hackett Fischer traces this early American regionalism to its origins in British regional differences. East Anglia and other counties on the east coast of England gave New England their linguistic peculiarities, vernacular architecture, religious intensity, and other folkways as diverse as child-naming patterns and local cuisine. Tobacco and slaves aside, the distinctive features of Chesapeake society derived in a similar way from the disproportionate recruitment of planter gentry from England's southern counties. The Delaware Valley, by contrast, drew its folkways from the midland and northern counties and contiguous portions of Wales that gave shape to the Quaker movement. Beginning about 1718 the American backcountry from New York south took most of its social character from the people of north Britain: the fifteen Ulster, Scottish, and north English counties that faced each other around the Irish Sea and shared both numerous cultural affinities and deep-seated hostilities. These people were used to border wars, and they brought their expectations to the American frontier, where they killed Indians—including peaceful Christianized tribes—with a zeal that shocked other settlers, particularly the Quakers.

These contrasts affected not only demographic and economic patterns and an extensive list of major folkways but also religion and government.

England contained both an established church and eloquent advocates for broad toleration, mostly among the dissenting population. By the end of the seventeenth century, toleration for Protestants had finally become official policy, and England emerged as one of the most pluralistic societies in Christendom. All these tendencies crossed the ocean, but they clustered differently in particular colonies. Until the middle of the eighteenth century most colonies were more uniform and, certainly in formal policy and often in practice as well, more repressive than the mother country. By 1710 the Church of England had become officially established from Maryland south through the islands, but Virginia was far less willing than England to tolerate dissent. In New England, by contrast, dissent became establishment, and the Anglican Church had to fight hard and occasionally share an awkward alliance with Quakers and Baptists to win any kind of public recognition. But in Rhode Island, Pennsylvania, and for most purposes the entire mid-Atlantic region, the triumph of toleration meant death for an officially established church. Only in the aftermath of the Great Awakening of the 1730s and 1740s did pluralism and toleration take firm hold throughout the entire continent.

Provincial governments also varied along the spectrum. Corporate forms predominated in New England, where virtually all officials were elected, and charters—whether officially granted by the Crown or unofficially adopted by the settlers—provided genuine antecedents for the written constitutions of the eighteenth century. As of about 1670 the rest of the mainland except Virginia had been organized under proprietary forms, devices whereby the Crown bestowed nearly the totality of its regal powers upon one or more "lords proprietors," who organized the settlement and, less easily, tried to secure the cooperation of whatever settlers they could attract. Because the Caribbean was the most viciously contested center of imperial rivalries, the West Indies in the 1660s and 1670s emerged as the proving ground for royal government, a form in which the Crown appointed the governor and the council (a body that both advised the governor and served as the upper house of the legislature); they in turn appointed the judiciary; and the settlers elected an assembly to join with the council and governor in making laws. Crown efforts to control these societies led by the end of the century to standardized sets of commissions and instructions and to the routine review of provincial legislation and the less frequent hearing of judicial appeals, both by the Privy Council. These routine procedures, especially as organized under the Board of Trade after 1696, largely defined what royal government was, and they could be exported to or imposed upon other settlements as well. But as late as 1678, Virginia remained the only royal colony on the mainland of North America.

The American continents had taken one exceptionally homogeneous people, the Indians (whose genetic similarities were far greater than those of the people of western Europe or even the British Isles) and transformed them over thousands of years into hundreds of distinct linguistic groups and tribal societies. As the emerging spectrum of settlement revealed, the New World was quite capable of doing the same thing to European intruders, whose own ethnic identities were but a few centuries old. The process of settlement could, in other words, create new ethnicities, not just distinct regions. By 1700 it had already magnified a select number of regional differences found within Great Britain. The passage of time seemed likely to drive these young societies further apart, not closer together. To take a single example, the institution of slavery, although it existed everywhere in at least a rudimentary form, tended to magnify regional contrasts, not reduce them. The main counterpoise to increasing diversity came not from any commonly shared "American" experience but from the expanding impact of empire. Only through closer and continuous contact with metropolitan England—London culture and the central government —would the colonies become more like each other.

During the last half of the seventeenth century, England discovered her colonies. Unlike the Spanish Empire, which subordinated trade to religious and political uniformity, the English government reversed these priorities. Parliament's interest in these tiny settlements derived overwhelmingly from its determination to control their trade, which, from the Restoration of 1660 to the American Revolution, was indeed the most dynamic sector of London's rapidly expanding commerce and thus a major factor in propelling London past Paris as Europe's largest city. Through a series of Navigation Acts, Parliament confined all trade with the colonies to English shipping (a major benefit to colonial shipbuilders as well), compelled major staple crops to go to Britain before leaving the empire for other markets, and tried to make Britain the source of most manufactures consumed in the colonies and the entrepôt for other European or Asian exports shipped to America. Despite ferocious resistance at first, these policies had achieved an extremely high level of compliance by the early eighteenth century. Later attempts to restrict colonial manufacturing and regulate the molasses trade were much less successful.

Crown efforts to assert political control over the colonies arose mostly out of frustration at early attempts to enforce these mercantilistic policies. Virginia had been a royal colony since 1624, but it drew almost no attention from the home government until Nathaniel Bacon's Rebellion of 1676–77 severely threatened the king's very considerable revenues from the tobacco trade. In subsequent years the Privy Council imposed on Virginia the same kind of close oversight that had emerged in the West Indies since 1660. New England attracted London's interest not because of its religious peculiarities—which seemed to sophisticated Londoners both anachronistic and rather embarrassing—but because it controlled more shipping than any other part of North America. Yankee skippers could undermine the Navigation Acts. To destroy that possibility, England revoked the charter of Massachusetts Bay in 1684, merged all the New England colonies into one enlarged Dominion of New England in 1686, added New York and East and West New Jersey to this union in 1688, and tried to govern the whole in an authoritarian manner without an elective assembly. The model for this experiment came from the autocratic proprietary colony of New York under James, Duke of York and brother of King Charles II. When the duke became King James II in 1685, he saw a way of salvaging these faltering efforts by imposing them on a broader constituency.

He got a revolution instead. After William of Orange landed at Torbay in November 1688 and drove James from England, Boston and New York copied this example and overturned James's representatives, Sir Edmund Andros and Sir Francis Nicholson respectively, in the spring of 1689. Maryland Protestants used the same occasion to overthrow the proprietary government of the Catholic Lord Baltimore. Thereafter, government by elective assembly was no longer in doubt. Massachusetts had to accept a new charter that imposed a royal governor on the province. Although the two leaders of the New York rebellion, Jacob Leisler and Jacob Milborne, were both hanged in 1691, the upheavals of 1689 permanently discredited autocracy in America. By the 1720s the Crown's only other option for effective control, the West Indian model of royal government, had become the norm on the continent as well. Only proprietary Pennsylvania and Maryland (the latter restored to the Calverts in 1716 when the fifth Lord Baltimore converted to Protestantism) and corporate Connecticut and Rhode Island held out from this pattern. Except for Pennsylvania, even they went formally bicameral, and all of them reorganized their court systems along stricter common-law lines. Throughout North America, government was acquiring structural similarities that it had never had in the seventeenth century.

This absorption into empire dramatically altered political culture in North America. The struggles surrounding the Glorious Revolution persuaded most Englishmen that they lived on an oasis of freedom in a global desert of tyranny. Eighteenth-century political ideology emerged as an effort to explain this anomaly and give it a solid historical foundation. In Britain and the colonies everyone in public life affirmed the "Revolution principles" of 1688, which always meant some variant of the triad of liberty, property, and no popery. The English gloried in their "mixed and balanced constitution," which prevented any monarch from corrupting a virtuous Parliament. This theme had both "court" (statist) and "country" (antistatist) celebrants and interpreters, and both crossed the ocean to America. Virginia and South Carolina became the purest embodiments of country ideology. They idealized the patriotic role of the truly independent planter-citizen and allowed virtually no holders of profitable public offices to sit in their assemblies. In New Hampshire, Massachusetts, and New York, by contrast, royal success usually depended—as in Great Britain—on the loyal support of a corps of these "placemen" in the lower house. The governor gained strength from defense needs, which were much greater than in the Chesapeake colonies. In this environment, country ideology became the creed only of a minority opposition through the 1750s, but its appeal would expand dramatically after 1763, when the entire imperial establishment came to seem a direct threat to provincial liberties instead of a bulwark for defending them.

Other forces also drew the separate parts of the empire closer together in the eighteenth century. Trade with Britain grew enormously. It did not quite keep pace with per capita population growth in the colonies from the 1690s to 1740, but thereafter it expanded even more explosively. Port cities became a dynamic part of the Atlantic cultural world in a way that had simply not been possible in the seventeenth century when New York City, for instance, regularly received only about half a dozen ships from Europe each year. By the mid-eighteenth century, with these arrivals almost daily occurrences, the colonists tended to divide into two distinct blocs: "cosmopolitans," who nurtured strong contacts with the rest of the world, and "localists," who were relatively isolated from such experiences and often suspicious of what outsiders wished to impose upon them.

Almost by definition, colonial newspapers reflected cosmopolitan values. They rarely reported local events in any systematic way. Instead, they informed their communities of what was happening elsewhere, particularly in Europe. The *Boston Newsletter*, established by an enterprising postmaster named John Campbell in 1704, became America's first successful paper. By the 1720s all the major northern ports had at least one, and by the 1750s three or four newspapers. South Carolina and Virginia each acquired one in the 1730s, and Maryland a decade later.

By the end of the 1760s every colony north of Delaware had also established its own college, but from Delaware south only William and Mary in Virginia provided higher education for the settlers. This difference was symptomatic. On the whole, northern colonies *replicated* the institutional potential of Europe. With New England setting the pace, they trained their own ministers, lawyers, physicians, and master craftsmen. Plantation societies *imported* them instead, even though white per capita wealth was considerably higher from Maryland south. Northern provinces were already becoming modernizing societies capable of internalizing the institutional momentum of the mother country. Southern provinces remained colonies, specialized producers of non-European crops and importers of specialists who could provide necessary services. But all mainland colonies grew at a prodigious rate. In 1700 they had only 250,000 settlers and slaves. That figure topped a million in the 1740s and two million in the late 1760s.

Among large events, both northern and southern colonies shared in the Great Awakening and the final cycle of wars that expelled France from North America. Some historians like to interpret the Awakening— a powerful concentration of evangelical revivals that swept through Britain and the colonies mostly between the mid-1730s and early 1740s—as a direct prelude to the American Revolution, but even though awakened settlers overwhelmingly supported independence in the 1770s, the relationship was never that simple or direct. "Old Lights," or opponents of the revivals, would provide both the loyalists and nearly all of the most conspicuous patriots. At no point in its unfolding did the Awakening seem to pit Britain against America. It divided both.

By 1763 Britain had emerged victorious from its midcentury cycle of wars with France, a struggle that pulled together most of the trends toward imperial integration that had been emerging since the 1670s. The last of these wars, what Lawrence Henry Gipson called the Great War for the Empire (1754–63), marked the fourth-greatest mobilization and the third-highest rate of fatality of any American military struggle from then to the present. (Only World War II, the Civil War, and the Revolutionary War mustered a higher percentage of the population; only the Civil War and the American Revolution killed a larger proportion of participants.) Despite widespread friction in the first three years, no other event could rival that war in the intensity of cooperation it generated between imperial and provincial governments. Both New Light and Old Light preachers saw nothing less than the millennium issuing from the titanic struggle. The result was more prosaic but still as unique as the effort. Great Britain expelled the government of France from North America and, in the Peace of Paris of 1763, asserted control over the entire continent east of the Mississippi except New Orleans, which France temporarily transferred to Spain along with the rest of Louisiana west of the great river.

The war left several ironic legacies. To North Americans who had participated, it seemed a powerful vindication of the voluntaristic institutions upon which they had relied for their success. To London authorities, it seemed to demonstrate the inability of North Americans to meet their own defense needs even under an appalling emergency. The British answer would be major imperial reforms designed to create a more authoritarian empire, capable of answering its vast obligations whether or not the settlers chose to cooperate.

Neither side noticed another heritage. During the struggle the Indians throughout the northeastern woodlands had shown a novel and intense distaste for shedding one another's blood. The Iroquois ideal of a league of peace among the tribes of the confederacy seemed to be spreading throughout the region, fired by universalist religious justifications for resisting any further encroachments from the settlers. The Delawares and Shawnees in the upper Ohio Valley provided most of this religious drive for Indian unity, which had a striking impact as early as Pontiac's war of resistance in 1763–64.

As events would show, it was too little, too late. But for the next half-century, this movement inflicted one disaster after another upon the settlers and subjected first the empire and then the United States to a rate of defense spending that would have enormous political consequences. Considering the limited resources upon which Indian resistance could draw, it was at least as impressive as the effort toward unity undertaken by the thirteen colonies themselves after 1763. It also suggests a final paradox. Without Indian resistance to seal British commitment to imperial reform, there might have been no American Revolution at all.

BIBLIOGRAPHY

Among many general and specialized studies available, these titles have been chosen to complement the topics discussed in the text.

The most satisfactory brief surveys of colonial America are Gary B. Nash, *Red, White, and Black: The Peoples of Early America*, 2d ed. (Englewood Cliffs, N.J.: Prentice-Hall, 1982), which emphasizes interracial influences; and Jack P. Greene, *Pursuits of Happiness: The Social Development of Early Modern British Colonies and the Formation of American Culture* (Chapel Hill: University of North Carolina Press, 1988), though it omits Indians entirely. Several collections of essays also provide outstanding introductions to the subject. Jack P. Greene and J. R. Pole, eds., *Colonial British America: Essays in the New History of the Early Modern Era* (Baltimore, Md.: Johns Hopkins University Press, 1984), summarizes current scholarship through the early 1980s on most relevant topics. Stanley N. Katz and John M. Murrin, eds., *Colonial America: Essays in Politics and Social Development*, 3d ed. (New York: Knopf, 1983), collects recent demographic, social, and political studies. Thad W. Tate and David L. Ammerman, eds., *The Chesapeake in the Seventeenth Century: Essays on Anglo-American Society* (Chapel Hill: University of North Carolina Press, 1979); Richard S. Dunn and Mary M. Dunn, eds., *The World of William Penn* (Philadelphia: University of Pennsylvania Press, 1986); David D. Hall, John M. Murrin, and Thad W. Tate, eds., *Saints and Revolutionaries: Essays on Early American History* (New York: Norton, 1984), stress, respectively but not always exclusively, the Chesapeake, the Delaware Valley, and New England.

Russell Thornton, *American Indian Holocaust and Survival: A Population History since 1492* (Norman: University of Oklahoma Press, 1987), carefully examines Indian demographics. Alfred W. Crosby, Jr., *The Columbian Exchange: Biological and Cultural Consequences of 1492* (Westport, Conn.: Greenwood Press, 1972), achieves a global perspective. Philip D. Curtin, *The Atlantic Slave Trade: A Census* (Madison: University of Wisconsin Press, 1969), has become indispensable. Important studies of settler-Indian relations include Francis Jennings, *The Invasion of America: Indians, Colonialism, and the Cant of Conquest* (Chapel Hill: University of North Carolina Press, 1975); James W. Axtell, *The Invasion Within: The Contest of Cultures in North America* (New York: Oxford University Press, 1985); and William Cronon, *Changes in the Land: Indians, Colonists, and the Ecology of New England* (New York: Hill & Wang, 1983). A good introduction to the Enlightenment debate on America is Henry Steele Commager and Elmo Giordanetti, eds., *Was America a Mistake? An Eighteenth-Century Controversy* (New York: Harper & Row, 1967).

Bernard Bailyn, *The Peopling of British North America: An Introduction* (New York: Knopf, 1985), provides a broad overview, but only his *Voyagers to the West: A Passage in the Peopling of America on the Eve of the Revolution* (New York: Knopf, 1986), fully reveals both the complexity of the subject and the extraordinary depth of his research. Edmund S. Morgan has written the best narrative history of any single colony in *American Slavery, American Freedom: The Ordeal of Colonial Virginia* (New York: Norton, 1975). The most significant recent studies of Chesapeake society are Allan Kulikoff, *Tobacco and Slaves: The Development of Southern Cultures in the Chesapeake, 1680–1800* (Chapel Hill: University of North Carolina Press, 1986); and Darrett B. Rutman and Anita H. Rutman, *A Place in Time: Middlesex County, Virginia, 1650–1750* (New York: Norton, 1984). On the Deep South, see Peter H. Wood, *Black Majority: Negroes in Colonial South Carolina from 1670 through the Stono Rebellion* (New York: Knopf, 1974). For the islands, see Richard S. Dunn, *Sugar and Slaves: The Rise of the Planter Class in the English West Indies, 1624–1713* (Chapel Hill: University of North Carolina Press, 1972). For colonial New England, the most interesting recent studies are David D. Hall, *Worlds of Wonder, Days of Judgment: Popular Religious Belief in Early New England* (New York: Knopf, 1989); Andrew Delbanco, *The Puritan Ordeal* (Cambridge, Mass.: Harvard University Press, 1989); and Carol F. Karlsen, *The Devil in the Shape of a Woman: Witchcraft in Colonial New England* (New York: Norton, 1987), an absorbing and innovative study of gender relations that uses witchcraft as a lens. The freshest community study is Christine Leigh Heyrman, *Commerce and Culture: The Maritime Communities of Colonial Massachusetts, 1690–1750* (New York: Norton, 1984). For an excellent introduction to the Delaware Valley settlements, see Barry Levy, *Quakers and the American Family: British Settlement in the Delaware Valley* (New York: Oxford University Press, 1988).

On regionalism, see David Hackett Fischer, *Albion's Seed: Four British Folkways in America* (New York: Oxford University Press, 1989). The best introduction to colonial politics remains Bernard Bailyn, *The Origins of American Politics* (New York: Knopf, 1968). For the midcentury wars, easily the most reflective study is Fred Anderson, *A People's Army: Massachusetts Soldiers and Society in the Seven Years' War* (Chapel Hill: University of North Carolina Press, 1984).